KT-130-523

WINCHESTER SCHOOL OF MISSION
06436

WRITING

IN THE DUST

WRITING
IN THE DUST

Reflections on 11th September

and its aftermath

ROWAN WILLIAMS

Hodder & Stoughton
LONDON SYDNEY AUCKLAND

Copyright © 2002 by Rowan Williams

First published in Great Britain in 2002

The right of Rowan Williams to be identified as the Author of
the Work has been asserted by him in accordance with
the Copyright, Designs and Patents Act 1988.

10 9 8 7 6 5 4 3 2 1

All rights reserved. No part of this publication may be
reproduced, stored in a retrieval system, or transmitted,
in any form or by any means without the prior written
permission of the publisher, nor be otherwise circulated
in any form of binding or cover other than that in which
it is published and without a similar condition being
imposed on the subsequent purchaser.

British Library Cataloguing in Publication Data
A record for this book is available from the British Library

ISBN 0 340 78719 8

Typeset by Avon Dataset Ltd, Bidford-on-Avon, Warks

Printed and bound in Great Britain by
Bookmarque Ltd, Croydon, Surrey

Hodder & Stoughton
A Division of Hodder Headline Ltd
338 Euston Road
London NW1 3BH

To all who met at Trinity
on 11 September 2001

CONTENTS

PREFACE

I must thank Judith Longman of Hodder and Stoughton for suggesting that there might be room for some reflections on the terrorist attacks of 11 September 2001, attempting to draw out how faith might begin to think and feel its way through the nightmare.

On 11 September, I was in a building used by the staff of Trinity Church, Wall Street, a couple of blocks away from the World Trade Centre, with a group of people planning to record several hours of discussion around issues of spirituality, to be broadcast through

Trinity's extensive and sophisticated educational programme. We were interrupted. We learned and received a very great deal from each other in the hours that followed, and these pages owe an enormous debt to all who shared that morning in that place – invited guests and speakers, production and office staff, and the others with whom we were thrown together. I hope I can say that what follows is in some sense from all of us. Writing about it is difficult. It has helped me and it may help you to think of it as the distillation of more than one voice.

After the 11th, *what are we prepared to learn?* That's the question to which I keep returning, and which fuels this meditation. Whatever the outcome of military action, whatever your views on the rights and wrongs of the reaction of the USA and its allies, that question remains for us. I'm conscious of using 'we' and 'us' a lot in these thoughts, meaning the whole of our Anglo-American world of which I'm not a detached observer gifted with superior morality any more, I suspect, than you are, reader. This 'we' needs, God knows, time and opportunity to grieve; but time and opportunity also to ask whether anything can *grow* through this terrible moment. I hope the answer is yes.

1

LAST WORDS

Last words. We have had the chance to read the messages sent by passengers on the planes to their spouses and families in the desperate last minutes; and we have seen the spiritual advice apparently given to the terrorists by one of their number, the thoughts that should have been in their minds as they approached the death they had chosen (for themselves and for others). Something of the chill of 11 September 2001 lies in the contrast. The religious words are, in the cold light of day, the words that murderers are saying to themselves to make a martyr's drama out of a crime. The non-religious words are testimony to what religious language is supposed to be about – the triumph of pointless, gratuitous love, the affirming of faithfulness even when there is nothing to be done or salvaged.

It should give us pause, especially if we think we are religious. You don't have to be Richard Dawkins to notice that there is a problem.

On the morning of 11 September 2001, I was getting ready to spend a day talking religious language with a group of clergy and spiritual directors. I am still thinking about what it meant to be interrupted like that; and to be presented with the record of a solemn and rich exhortation cast in evocative spiritual terms designed to make it easier for some people to kill others.

It isn't (say it now and get it over with) a problem about Muslims, about some kind of religiousness that is 'naturally' prone to violence. It's true that Islam seems to think differently about its language for God from the way Christians and Jews do; Muslims will regard what we say as too ambiguous, too larded with irony or paradox, self-indulgent in comparison with the sober directness of the Qur'an. But Christians at least have used their irony and paradox often enough to slip out from under the demands of justice or compassion. They have found plenty of ways to be absent from what they say, to play with commitment. The Jewish-Christian Bible is not a very straightforward set of texts, after all. No wonder post-modernism blossoms on post-Christian soil.

We'd better acknowledge the sheer danger of religiousness. Yes, it *can* be a tool to re-inforce diseased perceptions of reality. Muslim or not, it can be a way of teaching ourselves not to see the particular human agony in front of us; or worse, of teaching ourselves not to see ourselves, our violence, our actual guilt as opposed to our abstract 'religious' sinfulness. Our religious talking, seeing, knowing, needs a kind of cleansing.

Someone who is about to die in terrible anguish makes room in their mind for some-one else; for the grief and terror of someone they love. They do what they can to take some atom of that pain away from the other by the

4

inarticulate message on the mobile. That moment of 'making room' is what I as a religious person have to notice. It isn't 'pious', it isn't language about God; it's simply language that brings into the world something other than self-defensiveness. It's a breathing space in the asthmatic climate of self-concern and competition; a breathing space that religious language doesn't often manage to create by or for itself.

God always has to be rediscovered. Which means God always has to be heard or seen where there aren't yet words for him. Saying something for the sake of another in the presence of death must be one place of rediscovery. Mustn't it?

Careful. You can do this too quickly. It can sound as though you're gratefully borrowing someone else's terrible experience to make another pious point. And after all, not everyone dies with words of love. There will have been cursing and hysteria and frantic, deluded efforts to be safe at all costs when people knew what was going on in those planes. And would anyone want their private words of love butchered to make a sermon?

It proves nothing. But all I can say is that for someone who does believe, or tries to, the 'breathing space' is something that allows the words of religious faith for a moment not to be as formal or flat or self-serving as they usually are.

The morning after, very early, I was stopped in the street in New York by a youngish man who turned out to be an airline pilot and a Catholic. He wanted to know what the hell God was doing when the planes hit the towers. What do you say? The usual fumbling about how God doesn't intervene, which sounds like a lame apology for some kind of 'policy' on God's part, a policy exposed as heartless in the face of such suffering? Something about how God is there in the sacrificial work of the rescuers, in the risks they take? I tried saying bits of this, but there was no clearer answer than there ever is. Any really outrageous human action tests to the limit our careful theological principles about God's refusal to interfere with created freedom. That God has made a world into which he doesn't casually step in to solve problems is fairly central to a lot of Christian faith. He has made the world so that evil

7

choices can't just be frustrated or aborted (where would he stop, for goodness sake? He'd have to be intervening every instant of human history). They have to be confronted, suffered, taken forward, healed in the complex process of human history, always in collaboration with what we do and say and pray.

I do believe that; but I don't think you can *say* it with much conviction outside the context of people actually doing the action and the prayer. In the street that morning, all I had was words. I wasn't surprised that they didn't help. He was a lifelong Christian believer, but for the first time it came home to him that he might be committed to a God who could seem useless in a crisis.

Perhaps it's when we try to make God

useful in crises, though, that we take the first steps towards the great lie of religion: the god who fits our agenda. There is a breathing space: then just breathe for a moment. Perhaps the words of faith will rise again slowly in that space (perhaps not). But don't try to tie it up quickly.

Breathing. A bit paradoxical to talk about that. When we finally escaped from our building, it was quite hard to breathe normally in the street: dense fumes; thick, thick dust; a sort of sandstorm or snowstorm of dust and debris; large flakes of soft grey burned stuff falling steadily. In the empty street, cars with windows blown in, a few dazed people, everything covered in this grey snow. It can't have been silent. There must have been (I know there were) shouts, sirens;

a few minutes later, there was the inde-
scribable long roar of the second tower
collapsing. But I remember it as quiet;
the very few words spoken to each other,
the ghostliness of it all; surreal associations
with Robert Frost's lovely poem, 'Stopping
by woods on a snowy evening' ('The only
other sound's the sweep/Of easy wind and
downy flake'). Or a 'heart of the storm'
feeling.

In that time, there is no possibility of
thinking, of explanations, of resolutions. I
can't remember much sense of panic, much
feeling about the agony going on a couple of
hundred yards away, let alone much desire
for justice or vengeance. It was an empty
space. I don't want to forget that, as feeling
returns in various ways. We don't fully know

what goes on when, in the middle of terror or pain, this emptiness and anaesthesia set in (it happens in plenty of contexts). But somehow the emptiness 'resources' us. Not to run too fast to explore the feelings and recover the words seems important.

Simone Weil said that the danger of imagination was that it filled up the void when what we need is to learn how to live in the presence of the void. The more closely we bind God to our own purposes, use God to help ourselves avoid our own destructiveness, the more we fill up the void. It becomes very important to know how to use the language of belief; which is why the terrible simplicity of those last messages matters so intensely. And why also we have to tread so carefully in not making some sort of religious capital out of them. Ultimately, the importance of these 'secular' words has to stand as a challenge to anything comfortingly religious that we might be tempted to say. This is what human beings *can* find to say in the face of death, religion or no religion. This is what truly makes breathing space for others.

Words like 'transcendent' hang around uneasily in the background of my mind. Careful again. But that moment of pointless loving communication is the best glimpse many of us will have of what the rather solemn and pompous word means. I have to *begin* with this. I know I shall be feeling my way towards making some verbal shape out of it all in terms of my Christian faith, but there is nowhere else to start except with that frightening contrast: the murderously spiritual and the compassionately secular.

2

ANSWERING BACK

So much of this seems to oblige us to think about language.

The day after, I received a phone call from Wales, from one of the news programmes, and I faced a familiar dilemma. The caller started speaking to me in Welsh, which I understand without difficulty, but don't always find easy to use in an unscripted and possibly rather complex discussion. I had to decide. If I answered in Welsh, the conversation would go on in Welsh, and I had some misgivings about coping with it.

I am spoken to; I have some choices about how to answer. It seemed a telling metaphor at that particular moment. Violence is a communication, after all, of hatred, fear or contempt, and I have a choice about the language I am going to use to respond. If I decide to answer in the same terms, that is how the conversation will continue. How many times have you heard someone say, 'It's the only language they understand' to defend a violent reaction to violent acts? And perhaps before we reply, we should at least ask the kinds of question we might ask if we were addressed in a language we weren't quite sure about: Can I continue this conversation? Have I the will and resource for it?

At the same time, the question is a little unreal in some circumstances. The fantastic surge of violent energy needed to plan and carry through a colossal suicide attack is, fortunately, beyond the imagination of most of us. We can partly cope with thinking about the exchanges of conventional war, because we assume a measure of calculation on each side that is fairly similar. Increasingly (and this is something else we shall have to come back to) this is not what large-scale violence is like in our age. We face agents who don't seem to calculate gains and losses or risks as we do. It is not like the deceptively comfortable cold-war notion of a balance of terror.

A Palestinian woman brought up in New York, Suheir Hammad, wrote, one week after the 11th:

I do not know how bad a life has to break
   in order to kill.
I have never been so hungry that I willed
   hunger.
I have never been so angry as to want to
   control a gun over a pen.
Not really. Even as a woman, as a
   Palestinian, as a broken human being.
Never this broken.

And if not even as a woman, as a Palestinian,
what about the rest of us? What do we know?
   The truth is that if we respond violently
our violence is going to be a rather different
sort of thing. It is unlikely to have behind it
the passion of someone who has nothing
to lose; the terrible self-abandonment of
the suicidal killer, which is like a grotesque

parody of the self-abandonment of love. It is
not that we are 'naturally' less violent or more
compassionate. The record of European or
American military engagement should dispel
that illusion. But we are not acting out of
helplessness, out of the moral and imagina-
tive destitution that can feel it is *acting* at
all only when it is inflicting pain and
destruction.

The response of at least some people in
the face of deep injury, once feeling has
returned, is a passionate striking out; there
is something recognisable about the language
of Psalm 137 – 'let *their* children die horribly,
let *them* know what humiliation and exile are
like'. It is an honest moment; but for those of
us who are not totally helpless in terms of
internal or external resources it is only a

moment. We feel very uneasy when it seems as though there is a sustained effort to keep that level of murderous or revengeful outrage alive. The point at which we need to show more footage of collapsing towers or people jumping to their death, when we raise the temperature by injunctions never to forget – that is when something rather ambiguous enters in. We are trying to manipulate and direct the chaotic emotions of victims. There may be something like a dreadful innocence about the first surge of anger; there is no innocence about the deployment of images to try and revive it.

In a way, then, we're never going to be replying in quite the same language. We, with our military and financial resources, are never going to be exactly where the suicide bomber is. The car sticker may say 'Nuke Afghanistan', but we (collectively) are generally aware that this is more than a little unreal. We (collectively) have space to calculate gains and losses. There is some space between our feelings and our choices.

A pause to clarify one or two things. In the aftermath of 11 September, it was almost a cliché in some quarters to say that terrorism was bred by poverty and political helplessness, and there were two kinds of hostile response to this. There were those (usually on the right) who said that this was a false and sentimental account of the motivation of the killers: it was 'blaming the victim', indulging in facile anti-American feeling; it ignored the facts that the 'typical' al-Qaida activist seemed to be from a prosperous background, like Osama bin Laden himself, and that issues about American presence in Saudi Arabia or Israeli policy towards the Palestinians surfaced only after the atrocities as a sort of *post factum* rationalisation. No excuses: this is simply political evil, warped extremists seeking to maximise hurt against the USA. Then there were those on the left who began to talk about 'apocalyptic nihilism'. The atrocity is neither a despairing last resort nor a piece of horrible malignity, but a pulling down of the pillars over everyone's head, as if to provoke God himself into action or, as in nineteenth-century Russian anarchism, to provoke the forces of history into change.

There is something here of fair comment, because there has been coarse and facile anti-Americanism around, and there is an uncanny resonance with that kind of anarchism. But bombast about evil individuals doesn't help in understanding anything. Even vile and murderous actions tend to come from somewhere, and if they are extreme in character we are not wrong to look for extreme situations. It does not mean that those who do them had no choice, are not answerable; far from it. But there is sentimentality too in ascribing what we don't understand to 'evil'; it lets us off the hook, it allows us to avoid the question of what, if anything, we can *recognise* in the destructive act of another. If we react without that self-questioning, we change nothing. It is not true to say, 'We are all guilty'; but perhaps it is true to say, 'We are all able to understand *something* as we look into our-selves.'

The same with 'apocalyptic nihilism'. Nihilism breeds where things do not make sense; why and how they don't is again some-thing we can ask about, something where we can look for recognisable experience. The temptation is always to refuse the labour of this search; but if we refuse to undertake it, we say that there could never be any language at all in which to talk with some of our fellow human beings. It simplifies matters, but it certainly brings its own problems – not least for those who think of themselves as religious.

But to get back to the main issue: we have something of the freedom to consider whe-ther or not we turn to violence and so, in virtue of that very fact, are rather different from those who experience their world as leaving them no other option. But if we have that freedom, it *ought* to be less likely that we reach for violence as a first resort. We have the freedom to think what we actually want, to probe our desires for some kind of outcome that is more than just mirroring what we have experienced. The trouble is that this means work of the kind we are often least eager for, work that will help us so to understand another that we begin to find some sense of what they and we together might recognise as good. It means putting on hold our most immediate feelings – or at least making them objects of reflection; it means trying to pull apart the longing to re-establish the sense of being in control and the longing to find a security that is shared. In plainer English, it means being very suspicious of any action that brings a sense of release, irrespective of what it achieves; very wary of doing something so that it looks as if something is getting done.

It means acknowledging and using the breathing space; and also acknowledging and using the rage and vengefulness as a way of sensing a little of where the violence comes from. I'd better say it again: this is nothing to do with excusing decisions to murder, threaten and torment, nor is it a recommendation to be passive. It is about trying to act so that something might possibly change, as opposed to acting so as to persuade ourselves that we're not powerless.

This business of the language in which you

respond is, I think, what the Sermon on the
Mount is dealing with. It's so easy to repre-
sent the words of Jesus here as commending
passivity. You shake your head with a smile
and say, 'It's a wonderful ideal, it may even
be an ideal for individuals, but it has nothing
to do with the real world of communal and
political conflict.' But we're not reading
closely enough.

Jesus tells us to turn the other cheek and
walk the extra mile. The backhanded slap on
the right cheek, as careful readers have noticed,
is the kind of gesture that assumes no response at all; it's designed to be the end of the
story, because it simply affirms who is in
charge. The right of a soldier of the occupying
power to compel your labour is the same; once
you've done it, there is no more to be said.

The slave stands there rather than going away and slowly turns his head. The peasant looks at the soldier and speaks to him, saying, 'I choose to go another mile.' The world of the aggressor, the master, is questioned because the person who is supposed to take no initiatives suddenly does. As Gandhi discovered, this is very frightening for most of those who exercise power. It is action that changes the terms of the relationship, or at the very least says to the master that the world might be otherwise. It requires courage and imagination: it is essentially the decision *not* to be passive, not to be a victim, but equally not to avoid passivity by simply reproducing what's been done to you. It is always something of a miracle.

For the Christian, it is the miracle made

possible by the way in which God speaks. The story of Jesus understood as the 'speaking' of God to the world repeatedly brings this into focus. God speaks one language and human beings respond in another. God speaks to say, 'Don't be afraid, nothing will stop me welcoming you'; or to say, ' Be afraid only of your own deep longing to control me.' Human beings respond by fearing God and struggling to please him ('The hour is coming when anyone who kills you will think he is doing a holy duty for God', says Jesus in John 16:2); and by failing to fear the hunger within them to capture and manipulate God. The speech of God is silenced by death; but God is unable, it seems, to learn any other language, and speaks again in Jesus' resurrection.

So what are we going to say in what we do?

We could be saying, 'I must struggle to learn your language. I must hold on to what I've felt of your despair and strike back in the only language you understand. So I must train myself to look past the particular deaths of innocent people to make sure that my anger has adequate expression. I must work to keep up this pitch of energy until you have been silenced, and then perhaps I can start trying to relearn the language I used to speak.'

Or not, of course.

3

THE END OF WAR

We weren't completely sure at first, most of us, but it was of course violence we turned to. Not surprisingly because we felt, most of us, that there really was nothing else we could do. A long programme of diplomatic pressure, the reworking of regional alliances and a severe review of intelligence and security didn't feel like doing anything. There needed to be a discharge of the tension.

But what makes discharging tension attractive is that it is an act that has a beginning and an end. The attraction fades when we cannot see the end; and here lies the risk and frustration of the conflict that began in October. From the first, it was not at all clear what would count as victory in this engagement. The abolition of terrorism? No doubt, but what possible guarantee could there be that this had been achieved? The capture of Osama bin Laden? Perhaps, but this would not in itself begin to solve the underlying problems as to where terrorism comes from. There would be plenty to take his place if the fundamental balance of power did not change at all in the world; and the drama of a martyr's fate for bin Laden would give another turn to the screw. The overthrow of the Afghan government? We should need cast-iron certainty that the Taliban administration really bore responsibility for collusion with terror; and we should need what we conspicuously don't have, an alternative for the future of the country.

The conflict begins to become an embarrassment. It is *just* possible to deplore civilian casualties and retain moral credibility when an action is clearly focused and its goals are on the way to evident achievement. It is not possible when the strategy appears confused and political leaders talk about a 'war' that may last years. And there is a fine line between, for example, the crippling of military and aircraft installations and the devastating of an infrastructure with a half-formed aim of destroying morale. Combine that with the use of anti-personnel weapons such as cluster bombs, which ought to raise some serious questions (they have been described as aerial landmines in terms of their randomly lethal character), and the whole enterprise is tainted.

Tainted, because as soon as assaults on public morale by allowing random killing *as a matter of calculated policy* become part of a military strategy, we are at once vulnerable to the charge that there is no moral difference in kind between our military action and the terror that it attacks. This is not to reach for the too-easy rhetoric that says there is no distinction at all between the controlled violence of the state at war and the 'private' violence of terror (or indeed any unlawful killing); but the definition of what might be 'lawful' violence is always fragile. Self-defence, action against military personnel or officials of a hostile regime – these are the benchmarks that allow some principled distinctions to be drawn. From the point of view of a villager in Afghanistan whose family have died in a bombing raid, a villager who has probably never heard of the World Trade Centre, the distinctions between what the US forces are doing and what was done on 11 September will be academic.

To talk about lawful violence may seem odd, but law itself assumes that force is justified in some circumstances to defend a community's health and survival. But that health and that survival are themselves undermined when defended by indiscriminate or disproportionate means; the cost is too high. What we set out to defend has become corrupted in the process (and this remains the cornerstone of moral opposition to nuclear, chemical and biological armaments).

Something of this must apply to the international community. There is a high price to pay for allowing one nation to act in the name of a global campaign against terror while fudging the question of how in international law the matter might be brought to conclusion (in what court is a bin Laden to be tried?), and while claiming the freedom to determine its methods in the conflict without regard to the considerations we have just been looking at. Part of the process of putting in place an international 'policing' operation, designed to bring clearly identified criminals to trial and punishment, involves maintaining the trust of other nations, the confidence that it is more than the interest of one nation that will dictate the outcome.

A good deal of the moral capital accumulated during the first days and weeks was soon squandered. From a situation where Muslim nations, even Iran, expressed shock and sympathy, we came to a point where the shapelessness of the campaign led Muslims to ask whether there were any agenda other than the humiliation of an Islamic population. We may think this an outrageously wrong perception, but it becomes – or should become – a rather urgent factor in calculating how to restore a sense of lawfulness that would sustain some coherent action to punish, and how to secure a future that would be more settled and just for everyone.

Part of the problem is the fateful word 'war'. As soon as it was decided that the September atrocity was an act of war and that a 'war on terrorism' was to be undertaken, clarity disappeared. No one 'declared war' on Afghanistan; executive decisions were made to proceed with military action. At least in the UK, there is a sense of some public confusion. There is discussion of whether we are dealing with a 'just war', and the theoretical points are rehearsed (with varying degrees of accuracy) in the broadsheets. The language fosters the assumption that this is a conflict with a *story* to it – hopefully, a story with a happy ending, a victory for justice. But terrorism is not a place, not even a person or a group of persons; it is a form of behaviour. 'War' against terrorism is as much a metaphor as war against drug abuse (not that the metaphor isn't misleading there as well), or car theft. It can mean only a sustained policy of making such behaviour less attractive or tolerable. As we've been reminded often, this is a long job; but there is a difference between saying this, which is unquestionably true, and suggesting that there is a case for an open-ended military campaign.

I sometimes wonder whether we have actually seen the end of war as we knew it. Not that universal peace is about to break out; but what we once meant by war becomes ever less likely in our world. No longer do we see declarations of hostilities between sovereign states equipped with roughly comparable resources; no longer do we think of standing armies competing in the field. Gradually, since 1945, the shape of state violence has changed. There have been vicious conflicts around regional separatism (the Biafra conflict of the late 1960s, the USSR in Chechnya), interventions in neighbouring states to restore stability (Tanzania and Uganda) and, most noticeably, neo-colonial conflicts aimed at securing political domi- nance in often distant regions (Vietnam, the USSR in Afghanistan). More apparently con- ventional conflicts (Israel's defensive wars against Egyptian and Syrian aggression, the Iran–Iraq conflict) have been regularly over- shadowed by the irregular variety of these military adventures.

But with this goes an erosion of what once seemed straightforward virtues – heroism in defence of one's country or for the sake of justice, or even costly loyalty to one's allies under pressure. Ironically, these are the virtues now prized most in just those irregular groupings that cause us most anxiety. Terrorism survives not only on the oxygen of publicity but on its seductive offer to reinvent some of the most ancient and numinous of (generally male) aspirations. The mythology of the IRA and of al-Qaida alike promises to give your life and death the most immense significance – heroism, martyrdom – you take control of your destiny by pledging it to a cause that is beyond moral question, even beyond the possibility of ultimate failure. *You* will not die meaninglessly; that is reserved for your victims.

The comment is often made these days that we expect wars to be fought without casualties. Hence everyone's reluctance to commit ground troops to conflict, and the obsession with high-tech aerial bombardment.

'Obsession' is not too strong a word for the fantasy-laden researchers at the advancing edge of this technology ('Wars can be fought and won in half an hour'). Some attribute this fear of casualties to a culturally induced cowardice and indifference. But I wonder if this isn't too glib; we can make sense, as the terrorist or freedom fighter does, of death in a righteous or even invulnerable cause but, in a period after the end of war as we knew it, it is harder to understand our military engagements in these ways. And it's quite sensible not to want to die simply in a rather ambivalent police action in a foreign country (in the UK we have come to terms with our soldiers dying in Northern Ireland because that has seemed much more directly a matter of necessary and tragic defence).

The advent of superpowers has largely eradicated the old-fashioned kind of war; and the emergence of the USA as the only true surviving superpower has led some to speak not just of the end of war but of the end of history. What makes this not good news is that it obscures any idea that there are necessary but acceptable risks to be run if justice is to prevail; that loyalty to a community's vision may require the risk of failure in the short term, and of death itself. Brecht may have said, 'Happy the land that has no need of heroes' but, in his desire to keep at arms' length a false glorification of war, he missed the significance and attraction of a culture that at least allows some dignity to risk. When this is unrecognisable or in short supply in the ordinary discourse of a society, people will seek it out in strange places, hungry for danger, drama, meaning. We might cast a glance at our own backyards, at the fate of the young male in an environment of systemic poverty and unemployment. The least thoughtful are swept into petty-criminal subcultures (joy-riding, gangs); the more reflective may join the kind of pressure group, right or left, that promises feverish and dangerous activism. Some travel across the world in search of places and causes where heroism is possible.

It happens in our own societies; if we have a problem about grasping why al-Qaida activists so often come from prosperous backgrounds in moderately prosperous states, this is part of the answer there too. To become part of a threatened minority struggling at immense cost, even the risk of violent and horrible death, to defend justice or true faith is one way out of meaning-lessness (and it also explains a little of the overheated rhetoric that so often typifies internal religious debate these days; drama is another addictive drug in all sorts of con-texts). The technologically expert violence of a wealthy country against a wretchedly poor one illustrates the problem; it drives a solution still further away.

Yet at the same time, one of the main memories of those closest to the events of 11 September will probably be of the prosaic heroism of fire-fighters and police in Manhattan. Memories of that morning for me include the enormously careful calm of one of the building staff, trained as a volunteer fire-officer, deliberately talking us through the practical things to do next; and of the staff who were supervising the children's day care centre on the first floor, putting their own fear on hold while they reassured the children. Small examples of what was visible in much more costly ways outside, a couple of streets away. If we are to remember 11 September 2001, we had better remember this too; for example, that one fire-fighting unit in New York lost all its members that day. It puts a different perspective on heroism for a moment. It tells us that heroism is not always bound up with drama, the sense of a Great Cause, but is something about doing what is necessary for a community's health and security. For most of the time, this will be invisible; it is only in crisis that the habits slowly and even drearily formed over years emerge to make possible what can be seen only as extraordinary and selfless labours.

Some people, in other words, practise living in the presence of death; not courting dramatic immortality through a cause, but as part of what will or may be necessary to serve the social body. They are often likely to be ignored or belittled by articulate people, they lack the romance of those who take risks for the sake of giving their lives 'meaning'. Just as with the contrast between secular love and religious hate, we may well be sobered by the conjunction of heroism for the sake of 'martyrdom', with its attendant death and devastation, and the heroism of routine. In one way, we have been reacquainted with a local and unexciting heroism that we have ignored in our restless passion for drama.

Heroism may be more remote in a post-war world, but it has not disappeared. Perhaps we should ask how we as societies come to grips with the idea that there is something, some balance of equity and mutuality, to be sustained that may require us to train ourselves in becoming familiar with risk and death, so that we recognise what needs to be done in crisis. Without this, we either look desperately for where we can find dramatic outlets for our frustration, or else we dress up our adventures in an exaggerated rhetoric of struggle and suffering, with leaders appealing to our fortitude and endurance in a situation in which most of us are not going to be exposed to any risk at all. One effect of this, too, is the weary cynicism that overtakes our responses to political leaders. They deplore it loudly and quite understandably; but they might ask how much the forcing of a high moral tone contributes to it.

So can we stop talking so much about 'war', and reconcile ourselves to the fact that the punishment of terrorist crime and the gradual reduction of its threat cannot be translated into the satisfying language of decisive and dramatic conquest? Can we try thinking more about the place of risk and even loss in ordinary civil society; and about the moral resources needed to grapple with the continuing problems of shaping a lawful international order? Can we, for God's sake, let go of the fantasies nurtured by the capacity for high-tech aerial assault? As if the first move in any modern conflict had to be precision bombing? Experienced military personnel will insist on the differences of cultures, languages, terrain, infrastructure as factors that make it impossible to identify a single strategic plan as applicable everywhere. To try to reconceive our aims in terms of police action, the maintenance of international law, deprives us of some of the higher notes in the song, but it may be more to do with the reality we face.

And if we stopped talking about war so much, we might be spared the posturing that suggests that any questioning of current methods must be weakness at best, treason at worst.

We could ask whether the further destabilising of a massively resentful Muslim world and the intensifying of the problems of homelessness and hunger in an already devastated country were really unavoidable. We could refuse to be victims, striking back without imagination.

The hardest thing in the world is to know how to act so as to make the difference that *can* be made; to know how and why that differs from the act that only releases or expresses the basic impotence of resentment.

4

GLOBAL NEIGHBOURHOOD

One of the painfully contradictory elements in the first months of armed conflict was the observable fact that no one felt safer. The anthrax attacks in the USA and elsewhere created new levels of panic; learned articles on just how many kinds of biological weapon might be available to unspecified activists, or just how out of control the technology of nuclear weaponry might be, appeared with some regularity in the press.

It should have suggested to us that bin Laden and al-Qaida may be profoundly wicked people by most objective standards; but they are not identifiable with every evil, and their punishment, even their extermination, *will not in itself make us safer*. We long desperately to be told that the threat is over, but every new stage in the conflict makes such a reassurance less likely. The Oklahoma bombing shocked the USA yet, curiously, this internal assault did not make people afraid in the same way. It is almost as if an act of brutal violence from within, as it were, can be assimilated by the imagination as this cannot. *These* attackers are people we can't even speak to.

And yes, this may, I suppose, have something to do with a blank inability to see that a McVeigh (or for that matter a teenager rampaging with a shotgun in a school; is that less of a moral outrage?) represents the darkness and incomprehensibility that is within, the parts of our own context and system that we can't speak to; we can recognise and articulate trauma and fear when the attack comes from right outside. It's easier than coming to terms with the truth that there is something in our own common life that escapes reason or ordinary language.

But whatever is involved here, the fear and shock are pretty well unprecedented. Even in the UK, where terrorist violence has been more usual, anxiety is disturbingly high. It feels as though some kind of contract has been broken, some unspoken agreement guaranteeing that we in the North Atlantic world would be spared the majority human experience of insecurity and physical dread.

What Faustian contract did we think had been made on our behalf? How could we imagine that, in a shrinking world, we could for ever postpone being touched by that majority experience? In the global village, fire can jump more easily from roof to roof. Globalisation is not just an economic matter, the removal of pointless and archaic barriers to the movement of capital; not just a cultural matter, a McDonald's in every village in Papua New Guinea. It isn't even a matter of the free flow of information, so that images of the triumphant culture are everywhere (though that is so strong an element in the resentment of the non-Western world). All these things have one sobering consequence: suffering in one region is connected with action in another.

We want the goods that unrestricted markets can bring (unrestricted in the sense that no one other than the prosperous restricts them). But we have yet to come to terms with what the greater part of humankind believes to be the corollary of this: that the prosperous will be seen as the makers of poverty. In the global village, the one who becomes rich is seen as the thief of his neighbour's goods. We will rightly say that this is a crass oversimplification. Free capital movement benefits the expansion of markets, and so benefits all producers; there is more space for the producer to move into, more room for the small economy to grow.

But the response from the poorer economies will be stony-faced. Debt and its management consume the energies of depressed economies, and often result in political regression and instability; the great corporations operate their own protectionist policies, and are able to sustain them by the prevailing protocols on intellectual property rights (the patenting by companies of regional produce). Global economics is impressive in theory as regards its potential for regenerating local practice; but in reality it is seen as managed for the sake of those who are already victorious.

Every transaction in the developed economies of the West can be interpreted as an act of aggression against the economic losers in the worldwide game. However much we protest that this is a caricature, this is how it is experienced. And we have to begin to understand how such a perception is part of the price we pay for the benefits of globalisation. To pick up a point explored elsewhere, we have to see that we have a life in other people's imagination, quite beyond our control. Globalisation means that we are involved in dramas we never thought of, cast in roles we never chose. As we protest at how the West is hated, how we never meant to oppress or diminish other cultures, how we never intended to undermine Islamic integrity and so on, we must try not to avoid the pain of grasping that we are not believed.

Once again: this is not about Western guilt and non-Western innocence, not a recommendation to accept all that we are accused of. It is about acknowledging that it is hard to start any sort of conversation when your conversation partner believes, in all sincerity, that your aim is to silence them.

And now global involvement has come home, appallingly, to the West. The September atrocity was dreadful enough, but the anthrax panic reminds us that we are not dealing with an enemy far off, in a geographically confined location. Just as urban poverty in the 'developed' world, especially with its components of migrant workers and asylum seekers, has been described as the Third World on the doorstep, so we cannot any longer imagine that the world represented by al-Qaida is capable of being confined at a manageable distance.

The horror of being vulnerable to terrorist violence might open our eyes to the vulnerability that in fact underlies the whole globalisation process. It is harder to believe that our world is one in which the increase of wealth for a minority can be indefinitely projected without cost. Already the existence of wealthy residential developments surrounded by all the technological refinements of security in many of our cities tells us that the spiral of wealth is also a spiral of threat. For example, those economists who seem content to 'write off' the whole of the African continent for the foreseeable future will have to find something to say about the massive instability this will generate – for everyone.

So there is a particularly difficult challenge here, to do with making terms with our vulnerability and learning how to live with it in a way that isn't simply denial, panic, the reinforcement of defences. A good many who shared something of the experience of 11

September found themselves made aware that they were experiencing briefly what is the daily experience of people in other parts of the world, living under the threat of bombardment and random death. One of the things that we don't always appreciate about the Palestinian–Israeli deadlock is that both sides know what it is to be faced with regular terror. We may be a little less inclined now to wonder why they can't be 'reasonable' about the possibilities of settlement or reconciliation.

Indeed, that particular conflict points out the tragic fact that people who share a history of abuse and oppression may be completely unable to connect their stories with each other. Simply sharing the experience doesn't guarantee understanding, it seems. But the sudden and literally brutal discovery that there is no contract to protect people like us from death and danger, and the humiliation of not knowing even where the threat really comes from or when or how it may strike again – the sheer surprise may yet have its force in persuading us to make some connections.

Back to some earlier thoughts. The trauma can offer a breathing space; and in that space there is the possibility of recognising that we have had an experience that is not just a nightmarish insult to *us* but a door into the suffering of countless other innocents, a suffering that is more or less routine for them in their less regularly protected environments.

And in the face of extreme dread, we may

become conscious, as people often do, of two very fundamental choices. We can cling harder and harder to the rock of our threatened identity – a choice, finally, for self-delusion over truth; or we can accept that we shall have *no* ultimate choice but to let go, and in that letting go, give room to what's there around us – to the sheer impression of the moment, to the need of the person next to you, to the fear that needs to be looked at, acknowledged and calmed (not denied). If that happens, the heart has room for many strangers, near and far. There is a global hospitality possible too in the presence of death.

5

AGAINST SYMBOLS

Recognising common experience is the exact opposite of using someone else to fit with your agenda, using them to play out roles you have worked out and assigned. We have been very resourceful in this over the centuries. Christians have conscripted Jews into their version of reality and forced them into a role that has nothing to do with how Jews understand their own past or current experience – what one scholar called 'using Jews to think with'. In the Middle Ages, Muslims too were made to play a part in the drama written by

Christians, as a kind of diabolical mirror-image of Christian identity, worshipping a trinity of ridiculous idols. This was a distortion nurtured by popular religion, of course; responsible theologians studied the Qur'an and knew better. But those very writers who were so careful not to parody Islam were also capable of calmly and authoritatively writing nonsense about women; it would not have occurred to them that there was a Christian principle involved in listening to what women had to say about themselves . . .

And yes, of course, Jews and Muslims cherished equally bizarre beliefs about Christianity at times. They, like us, needed to assert some kind of control over the stranger, the other, by 'writing them in' in terms that could be managed and manipulated. What happens is that the stranger is assigned a meaning, a value, in the dominant system. When, as with Christians and Jews in Europe, this is allied to a hugely disproportionate distribution of power, the effects are dreadful.

'Using other people to think with'; that is, using them as symbols for points on your map, values in your scheme of things. When you get used to imposing meanings in this way, you silence the stranger's account of who they are; and that can mean both metaphorical and literal death. Death as the undermining of a culture, language or faith and, at the extreme, the death of tyranny and genocide. I have been using religious examples, but it isn't essentially a failing of religion itself. The collective imagination needs the outsider to give itself definition – which commonly means that it needs somewhere to project its own fears and tensions. The history of modern Europe's attitudes to the non-Western world, the history of what has come to be called 'Orientalism' – the imagining of the East as a mysterious opposite to the West, both devilish and subtly attractive – spells this out clearly.

Living realities are turned into symbols, and the symbolic values are used to imprison the reality. At its extreme pitch, people simply relate to the symbols. It is too hard to look past them, to look into the complex humanity of a real other.

The World Trade Centre and the Pentagon were massively obvious symbols of American dominance, both economic and military. To target them was clearly a blow against that entire system of dominance. The trouble is that, while burning the Stars and Stripes in a demonstration is one thing, the Twin Towers and the Pentagon were inhabited buildings; they may have been 'natural' symbols, but the people in them were not (people never are). It is a point that was missed even by some commentators who wrote as if the Trade Centre were entirely full of prosperous bond traders and the Pentagon full of military strategists. It's easy to forget cleaners and maintenance staff, the anonymous and necessary background for large enterprises like these; many of them people of uncertain civic status (how many illegal immigrants died on 11 September? We are not going to know because they had no official existence) – the

Third World on the doorstep of Manhattan and Washington.

But even if the buildings had been full of professionals working for American domination, not even then could we say that these people could be reduced to symbols: they had families, hobbies, a 'hinterland' of human life not consumed in professional identities. It is always people who suffer and are killed, not symbols. When we strike out at a symbol such as a flag, we hurt nothing except perhaps the self-esteem of those who use the language of which it's a part. When we decide to treat people as symbols, the story is different.

But the effect of this symbolic outrage against the tokens of dominance has been to populate our own world with more symbols. The Muslim world is now experiencing – as it has for some time, but now with so much more intensity – that 'conscription' into someone else's story that once characterised the Church's attitude to Jews. And individual 'strangers' in the UK and USA (including people born and raised in these countries) who are recognisable by speech, pigmentation, dress or whatever are discovering what it is like to be loaded with meanings by the majority around them, to be forced into the role of 'potential terrorist'. Muslim mothers with small children are attacked or insulted in the streets; Sikhs are abused as Muslims (i.e. enemies) because anyone in a turban is a terrorist. Some have already been killed. And on the other side of the world, it is not only flags that are being burned; presumably the Christians massacred in Pakistan in October

71

were seen as 'signs' of Western (i.e. American) presence and power.

So the drama continues, both sides engaging in the same terrible simplifications, striking against symbols that have closed around the flesh and history of human beings. And the whole process of turning people into symbols in this murderous way has its roots in our shared inability to face the fact, already mentioned, of division, failure and ambiguity within our systems. There is, I've said, a certain relief in being able to point to a clear outside agency responsible for terror (we should not forget the assumption instantly made after the Oklahoma bombing that it was the work of Muslim extremists). But there are a good many Muslims who will also admit that the

USA is equally a convenient scapegoat for the political dysfunctionalism of much of the Islamic world today, an excuse for not addressing the internal problems of some despotic and corrupt regimes.

Once the concreteness of another's suffering has registered, you cannot simply use them to think with. You have to be patient with the meanings that the other is struggling to find or form for themselves. Acknowledging the experience you share is the only thing that opens up the possibility of finding a meaning that can be shared, a language to speak together.

I'm not sure, but perhaps this is something of what some of our familiar Christian texts and stories point us towards. In the ninth chapter of the Gospel of John, Jesus encounters a man blind from birth, and his disciples encourage him to speculate on why he should suffer in this way. Who is being punished, the man or his parents? They are inviting Jesus to impose a meaning on someone's suffering within a calculus that assumes a neat relation between suffering and guilt.

Jesus declines; guilt is irrelevant, and all that can be said is that this blindness is an opportunity for God's glory to become manifest. The meaning is not in the system being operated by the disciples, but in the unknown future where healing will occur. As the story proceeds, we see how the fact of healing becomes a problem in turn, because it does not fit into the available categories; an outsider, a suspected heretic, has performed it. The blind man is again faced with people, this time the religious authorities, who want him to accept a meaning imposed by others, and he resists. It is this resistance, which proves costly for him, that brings him finally to faith.

What should strike us is Jesus' initial refusal to make the blind man's condition a *proof* of anything – divine justice or injustice, human sin or innocence. We who call ourselves Christian have every reason to say no to any system at all that uses suffering to prove things: to prove the sufferer's guilt as a sinner being punished, or – perhaps more frequently in our world – to prove the sufferer's innocence as a martyr whose heroism must never be forgotten or betrayed. If this man's condition is to have a symbolic value – and in some sense it clearly does in

the text – it is as the place where a communication from *God* occurs – the opening up of
something that is not part of the competing
systems operated by human beings.

I want to say that it is only here, with the
renunciation of all our various ways of
making suffering a weapon or a tool of ideol-
ogy, that we are going to learn how to grieve
properly. Of course, we just grieve anyway,
'properly' or not; but where does our grief
take us? And what do we mourn for? If, as St
Augustine says in his *Confessions*, we can fail
to 'love humanly', then surely we can also
fail to grieve humanly, to grieve without the
consolation of drama, martyrdom, resentment and projection. Are there words for
grief that can make us more human, so that
we mourn, not just for ourselves but for those

whose experience we have come to share, even for those whose moral poverty is responsible for murder and terror?

What use is faith to us if it is only a transcription into mythological jargon of the mechanisms of that inhuman grief that grasps its own suffering to itself as a ground of justification and encloses the suffering of others in interpretations that hold it at a safe distance?

And Christian faith? Can we think about our focal symbol, the cross of Jesus, and try to rescue it from its frequent fate as the banner of our own wounded righteousness? If Jesus is indeed what God communicates to us, God's language for us, his cross is always both ours and not ours; not a magnified sign of our own suffering, but the mark of God's

work in and through the deepest vulnerability; not a martyr's triumphant achievement, but something that is there for all
human sufferers because it belongs to no
human cause.

Breathing spaces again: if the cross is what
we say it is, it requires that kind of hesitation,
that kind of silence.

Epilogue

I called this reflection *Writing in the Dust* for many reasons. The obvious one is the sheer physical recollection of that dense, grey atmosphere in the streets; the soft fall of ash and paper; the gritty, eye-stinging wind. All that is written here begins in the dust of the streets that morning.

And then, writing in the dust is writing something that won't last, something exposed to dissolution; like the sand mandalas made by Tibetan monks for festivals, made to be broken up. This isn't a theology or a programme for action, but one person's attempt to find words for the grief and shock and loss of one moment. In the nature of things, these words won't last, and I need to acknowledge and accept that, and hope only that they may help to take forward someone else's mourning.

But lastly, another picture from the Gospel of John evoked for me by all this, from the stray story of Jesus and the woman taken in adultery that is preserved, rather improbably, in John 8. When the accusation is made, Jesus at first makes no reply but writes with his finger on the ground. What on earth is he doing? Commentators have had plenty of suggestions, but there is one meaning that seems to me obvious in the light of what I think we learned that morning. He hesitates.

He does not draw a line, fix an interpretation, tell the woman who she is and what her fate should be. He allows a moment, a longish moment, in which people are given time to see themselves differently precisely because he refuses to make the sense they want. When he lifts his head, there is both judgement and release.

So this is writing in the dust because it tries to hold that moment for a little longer, long enough for some of our demons to walk away.